LET'S TAKE THE BUS

For Emma Deaso

First Steck-Vaughn Edition 1992

Copyright © 1989 American Teacher Publications

Published by Steck-Vaughn Company

Library of Congress number: 89-3603

Library of Congress Cataloging in Publication Data.

Carlson, Judy.
  Let's take the bus/Chris Economos; illustrated by Steve McInturff.

  (Real readers)
  Summary: Five foolish animal friends have trouble getting home on the bus.
  [1. Buses—Fiction. 2. Animals—Fiction.] I. McInturff, Steve, ill. II. Title. III. Series.
PZ7.E2125Le   1989   [E]—dc19   89-3603

ISBN 0-8172-3500-0   hardcover library binding

ISBN 0-8114-6702-3   softcover binding
        8 9 0   00 99

LET'S TAKE THE BUS

by Chris Economos
illustrated by Steve McInturff

RSVP
RAINTREE
STECK-VAUGHN
PUBLISHERS
The Steck-Vaughn Company

Austin, Texas

"It is time to go home," said Elephant. "But it is too hot to walk."

"How can we get home?" said Bear.

"We can hop!" said Kangaroo.

"Yes, we can hop home!" said Rabbit and Frog.

"If it is too hot to walk," said Elephant, "it is too hot to hop!"

"This is what we will do," said Bear. "We will take the bus!"

"Let's take the bus!" they all said.

The bus came. Elephant and Bear got on. Kangaroo and Rabbit got on. Frog got on, too. They all sat down.

"Let's go," they all said.

CREAK, CREAK. The bus did not go!

The bus driver said, "The bus will not go! You will have to walk home."

"It is too hot to walk," said Elephant. "We want to take the bus. I can help. I will get off and push."

Elephant pushed the bus.

Push, push. CREAK, CREAK. The bus did not go!

The bus driver said, "The bus will not go! You will have to walk home."

"It is too hot to walk," said Bear. "We want to take the bus. I can help. I will get off and push."

Bear pushed Elephant, and Elephant pushed the bus.

Push, push. CREAK, CREAK. The bus did not go!

The bus driver said, "The bus will not go! You will have to walk home."

"It is too hot to walk," said Kangaroo. "We want to take the bus. I can help. I will get off and push."

Kangaroo pushed Bear. Bear pushed Elephant, and Elephant pushed the bus.

Push, push. CREAK, CREAK. The bus did not go!

The bus driver said, "The bus will not go! You will have to walk home."

"It is too hot to walk," said Rabbit. "We want to take the bus. I can help. I will get off and push."

Rabbit pushed Kangaroo. Kangaroo pushed Bear. Bear pushed Elephant, and Elephant pushed the bus.

Push, push. CREAK, CREAK. The bus did not go!

The bus driver said, "The bus will not go! You will have to walk home."

"It is too hot to walk," said Frog. "We want to take the bus. I can help. I will get off and push."

Frog pushed Rabbit. Rabbit pushed
Kangaroo. Kangaroo pushed Bear.
Bear pushed Elephant, and Elephant
pushed the bus.

Push, push. CREAK, CREAK, CREEEEAK!

The bus began to go!

The bus driver said, "Good! Good!
Keep pushing. The bus is going."

Frog pushed Rabbit. Rabbit pushed
Kangaroo. Kangaroo pushed Bear.
Bear pushed Elephant, and Elephant
pushed the bus.

They pushed and pushed and pushed.
They pushed the bus up the hill. They
pushed the bus down the hill.

They pushed the bus all the way home.

"It was good to take the bus!" said Bear.

"Yes," said Kangaroo.

"Yes," said Rabbit and Frog.

"Yes," said Elephant. "It was too hot to walk!"

Sharing the Joy of Reading

Beginning readers enjoy reading books on their own. Reading a book is a worthwhile activity in and of itself for a young reader. However, a child's reading can be even more rewarding if it is shared. This sharing can enhance your child's appreciation—both of the book and of his or her own abilities.

Now that your child has read **Let's Take the Bus**, you can help extend your child's reading experience by encouraging him or her to:

- Retell the story or key concepts presented in this story in his or her own words. The retelling can be oral or written.

- Create a picture of a favorite character, event, or concept from this book.

- Express his or her own ideas and feelings about the characters in this book and other things the characters might do.

Here is an activity you can do together to help extend your child's appreciation of this book: **Let's Take the Bus** is a fantasy story, featuring some funny animal friends who talk and act like people in some ways. You and your child can discuss other fantasy books, television shows, or movies you know in which animals talk and act like people in some ways. Then you and your child may want to reread a favorite fantasy story together or select a new one from your local library.